REET N

Pearl
&
Ash

Limited Special Edition. No. 5 of 25 Paperbacks

After the huge success with her debut book, a memoir – *Worth It!* – Reet Mann has yet again impressed her readers across the globe by writing a completely different genre poetry. Teasing the silky threads of love, wrapped in the linen of hurt and pain, she transforms emotions of weakness into strength. She doesn't stop here, she goes into exploring the wools of inspiration, leading to the velvets of spirituality. She never fails to surprise us!

Reet Mann's

Pearl & Ash

AUSTIN MACAULEY PUBLISHERS™
LONDON • CAMBRIDGE • NEW YORK • SHARJAH

Copyright © Reet Mann (2019)

The right of **Reet Mann** to be identified as author of this work has been asserted by her in accordance with section 77 and 78 of the Copyright, Designs and Patents Act 1988.

All rights reserved. No part of this publication may be reproduced, stored in a retrieval system, or transmitted in any form or by any means, electronic, mechanical, photocopying, recording, or otherwise, without the prior permission of the publishers.

Any person who commits any unauthorised act in relation to this publication may be liable to criminal prosecution and civil claims for damages.

A CIP catalogue record for this title is available from the British Library.

ISBN 9781528929165 (Paperback)
ISBN 9781528965767 (Epub e-book)

www.austinmacauley.com

First Published (2019)
Austin Macauley Publishers Ltd
25 Canada Square
Canary Wharf
London
E14 5LQ

This is for everyone who deserted me.
Had you not abandoned me, I wouldn't have written this book.

I am thankful to each one of you!

Guritta, I love you!

Sans, thanks for being there.

Love

To draw love,
don't do love...
be love!

"A new feeling and a new word,
I felt as it was a new world;
the hues in rainbow were never so bright,
all wrongs suddenly became right!

So amiable the things became,
as if despairs to me never came;
your deep limpid eyes,
which have been epoch of my life,
can narrate the story to the world,
O' how I learnt the new word.
The word unsaid but promises completely,
bo be ad infinitum in fidelity.

As choir is to chord, in the similar way,
for all my withered past, you are a nosegay.
A sight of yours makes me bloom,
thus, arouses an ardent wish to be with you soon!

Baroquely intense, yet so simple;
in the dark even my wish twinkles.
It changed my life and sense to give,
the word is love, now in which I live...

I smile, these days,
now I see some dreams—to chase,
since you came in my life,
I have lived again.
Only if I may dare say…
I can just give you my faith,
voicing—you are special in all your ways,
I stand by you, whatever it takes.

The moments spent in one another's arms,
have timeless charms,
you usually seal your lips
whenever I ask…
but the pair of black eyes—
O' the eyes…
in me they confide,
reveal you are mine…
trusting your lady, I am,
believing in you as my man…

As the coffee brews on a cold winter morning,
and the icy walls turn browner and warmer,
validating the beginning of something stronger,
quite similarly...
you bring flavour into my life...!

My heart now is used to the scene,
skipping a beat...
only at the citation of your name,
I close my eyes and the lashes mist,
lips further seal...

I turn away and shy;
thinking, when you look at me into the eye,
in that moment, am sure to live and die,
both at the same time...
in wait for your footsteps to arrive...

The dew when drops from the petal,
knowing to come and touch it the next day,
not worrying if the flower is plucked this noon...
or the floret falls in love with the moon...
that devotion in faith,
I long and await...

Come to me, only
if you can hold me
in pain and grief...
if you can stand by me...
only for you,
not for the sake of me...

The globe keeps revolving,
but you find yourself standing still...
when you experience it;
love is the power
that changes the course of anything,
yes, even axis...

Quest to answer the enigma,
fosters a will to reveal a mystical charisma;
all paths in an aesthetic view,
yet what eyes search infinitely—it's only you!

Innocent smile and a crude look,
all it takes to give me a woe;
no words said but a silent cue,
what means eternity to me—it's only you!

Tranquillity in him of a kind,
uncaptured, caught by sight;
essence of leaves is the dew,
but to me—it's only you!

Never could I fathom the magic,
which elated my life joyous from tragic;
the unknown, cryptic slyly grew,
I now do avow—it's only you...

What is mixed in water
can't be extracted back from it...
likewise, you can't undo love...
it is dissolved in you—forever...

To taste love,
you must be ready to offer
the open flesh of your heart…
either to be pierced and stabbed,
or to be cherished…
you sure will favour love
either way…

Love is like a flame,
it illuminates you and your surroundings...
embrace the feeling,
since you are already in the state;
do not seek it in return,
you are losing the freedom...
for it can be as great as you want
while bestowing it,
you can't control the measure while receiving...

No, don't disparage it...
I beseech...
do not put it into words,
your eyes have said enough...
let the desire of your gaze sink in,
let me take pride in what it is drinking...

The brown silk cascade,
when covers your face...
the breeze comes to my rescue,
through the gaps, I now manage the view.
I see your lips curved in a smile,
my eyes feel light and the soul—bright...

Your touch completes me...
you present me to me...
illusions become true,
I gather the missing link—
it always was you...

Through the cracked skin
and the wrinkled face...
I still see radiance stay,
the fair art of every play...

Love is the reflection
of one's satisfaction,
in recognising passion
in thou...
the echo towards you
will then flow...

If you know not love...
you see nothing of worth...!

I seek no proof
of having you,
it's the peace I procure
knowing deep down,
you belong here—is quite enough...

I laugh, when they say
you can't be mine,
these days I hear it a lot,
naïve—they don't absorb, alas;

I don't mean to mock
but releasing the smog…
when the hearts talk
and eyes lock,
you are in me and
I am yours…

As the drops of honey
trickle over the ground…
barren feels the passion
in part by measure…
go ask her,
she feels fulfilled…

While setting your love free
you don't have a choice…
it is an inevitable price
all lovers have to pay…
for love is a mighty dear taste
afforded by a few
and worthy of even rare…

If I am to be drowned,
please be it in your love,
the air suffocates me...

Hold me...I feel shielded
in the armour of your arms...
now take me to any field or arena,
I will keep you safe...

I meditate in your words,
and reach the divine
relishing your smile…
takes me closer
inch by inch to the light…

Pain

There is a lot to conquer
do not underrate,
concede the power
that resides in pain.

I wish you were here,
but then, the wish alone is better than having you,
you mesmerize me now, only in my thoughts,
it is the power of my imagination,
it has nothing to do with you!

Some days, I crave
to be dipped in you;
to be savoured by you,
then the desire evades
only remembering the real you.

The empty pillow by my side
doesn't make me lonely,
it only reminds me
my worth.
I become more desirable than I ever was...

The pair of eyes set on me
I wonder what it sees—
the creamy flawless skin
or the shredded soul...
and does it dare to peek
at my undefeated will?

You can throw the filth here,
even better—disgrace me,
I become purer with every attempt of insult.
only wish I could cleanse the mirror,
so you could see your true reflection.

Elated you felt, when I kept giving
so much that nothing of me remained in me.
Now that I leave, I intact you whole,
I won't claim the part of me that you kept,
that's my last present to you,
since you were never complete without me.

Your smile reminds me
nothing is real;
no heart, soul, pain, sorrow, love, ache.
O dear, nothing is real,
and then...I smile!

I waited to be valued
belittling just that...

Giving too much for too long,
inevitably flows into a too painful consequence.

The one who betrays those
who could do anything loving them
are the unfortunate paradox,
acting the trigger and victim
of their own catastrophe...

You conquered my skin, even my soul,
you reigned me—only because I let you!
Ruining your gifted empire, you forgot—
if I could bestow myself upon you;
I can rebuild myself—glorious than ever…

I walked at your pace,
as long as you wished.
as soon as I paused to catch a breath
I was labelled a traitor!
Still trying to catch the same breath I paused for,
other than that, I breathe fine!

They may call it success,
a few even say it's the glory;
what all I did was...
told you my story.

I know not art,
neither do I master the skill.
Just sewing a wounded heart,
slowly, learning the drill.

You were too shallow
to have your interests weighed over mine,
had you sneaked at my interests prudently,
you would have uncovered and shied;
yours but only yours, were sheltered
in the deep layers of mine.

Amidst the applaud,
I still miss your nod...

Either I want you full,
or I shall pass
I don't do life in halves.

They all look at me,
yet, I wait for the same pair of eyes.
It is gratifying sometimes,
to be tangled in aching twines.

If only you had loved me
deep enough,
if only you had loved me hard enough...
if only had it been just enough.

I walk away with nothing but my honour,
and some slice of blotted soul, tarnished spirit
and oh, the tattered heart...
still beating!

I admire your courage
to lie…
looking straight into my eyes,
you could tell all the whys
knowing what you were hiding,
I let you tell it anyway
so one of us still feels high,
for I was smashed to the floor
just admiring your courage to lie
I seldom listened to your words…
your eyes still into mine,
usually would suffice.

What's the noise?
was it expensive that smashed?
Has the shard cut deep?
Or someone bleed?
Hope it's not the piece of art?
"Nah!" I answered...
"It's only my heart!"

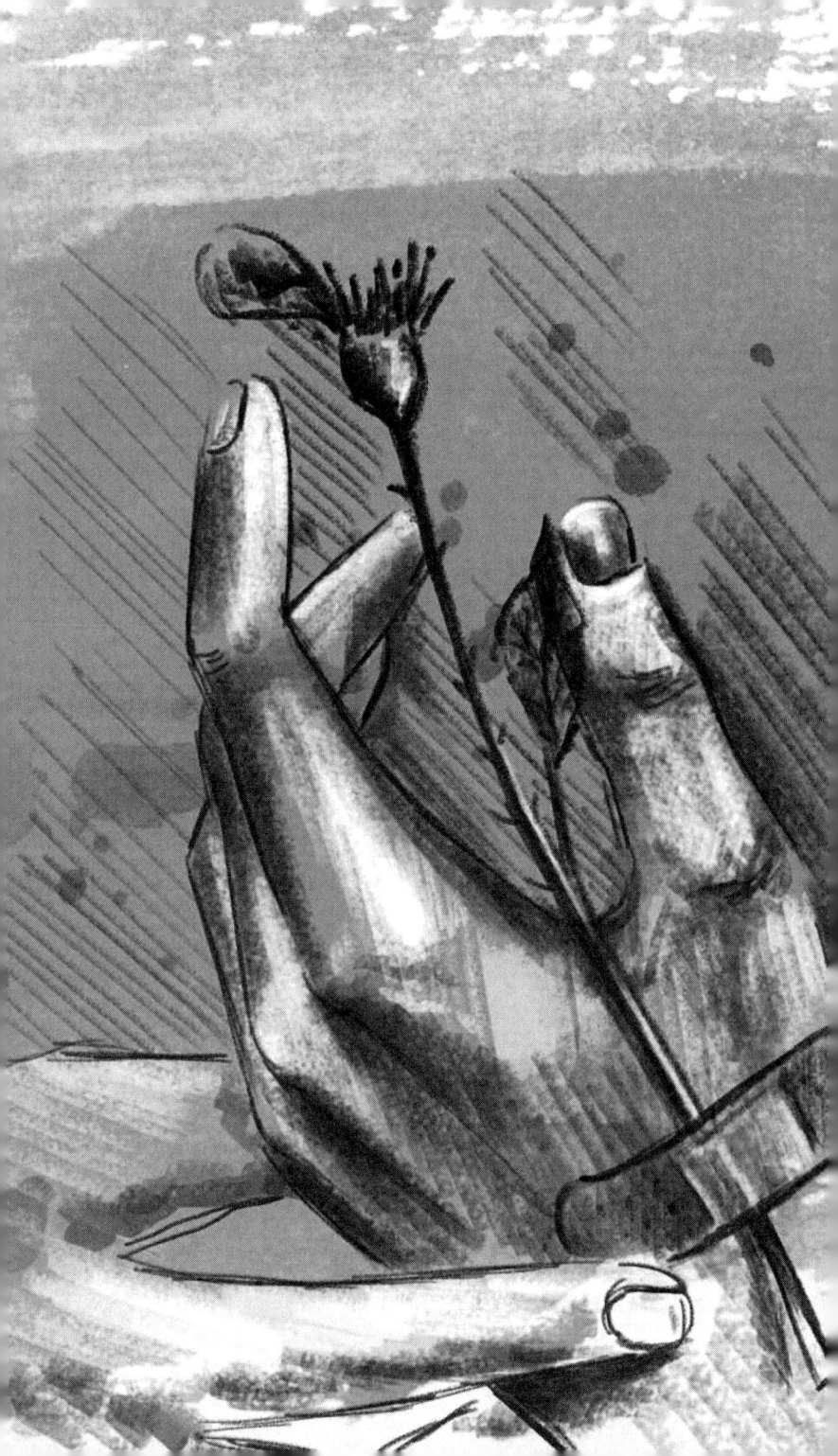

It's good to carry a broken heart,
it teaches you a few lessons…
for one…you are done with the aching track
and then, only you have to put the bits back,
by now you know, no one could care less,
and here is a critical arc…
keep it well under guard.

Life is not what I am living…
it's what I wanted to live;
listening to the beats of your heart,
dancing to its rhythm!

I am living…
hauling a soothing twinge within,
and a sinking air,
with limbs feeling light
lifeless, yet alive…

It's the truth,
I could never match your love…
I second the charge.
while you were fancying me with stance,
I have been worshipping you…
all along…
for I know not love
sans devotion.

Inspiration

Summits are demanding,
well, so is life;
let's climb it anyway...

You are the answer to your quest,
your own escape,
the caress on the nape,
strong wind—when there is need

continued...

to shed that leaf...
gentle frost—on your own petals;
you are the cure to your own wound,
derive thyself from your own crude...

There is no bigger power in the world displayed, when a woman uplifts another.

"Believe in yourself to make the world believe you."

I dream...
fly and very high,
I know when to rest
in my nest;
I am my own anchor,
and my own sail!

When you hit the rock-bottom,
brace yourself...
your time has come,
go fly...
awaits you, the entire sky!

The downfalls have plenty to teach,
people remain out of reach

continued...

for interests of others in you when breach,
but that's when the inner self and you greet!

Dear Phoenix, you are not alone...
I have been through it with you,
we are only born when burnt to the core!

Smile often,
if not in ecstasy, bliss or glee;
it will give you freedom
from the waiting!

There is no stopping you,
to reach the peak
it's the first step towards the creek
that poses magnitude,
for the rest of the hike
shed the baggage and
climb...weighing light...

Don't quit
until you have nothing left to put in!
For you are too close
pursuit itself is going to give in...

Merciless, when comes to test,
you are left all alone to impress;
act upon what you believe is earnest,
never mind, what think the rest
you are your virtual best...

Let it go,
feel the flow and sway,
believe me...they tried,
but there is no other way...

If someone choses else over you,
just forgive the poor soul;
with the ocean awaiting,
it's the mirage they choose...
what in the story,
did the ocean have to lose?

Continued...

You can't be depleted,
you can't be forgotten,
you stay there, with arms open,
they must be paying the toll
my dear ocean...
just forgive the poor soul...

The burnt desires,
when abate into ash;
in those dusty, lose ties
comes the powerful trice
the treasure is then exposed...
believe...speak no words...
rummage the ash,
that's where you will find the pearls...

If you feel the love,
and still ache for me...
we shall meet,
I have but left it
on you, for this promise to keep.

I have kept them all,
the ones I made,
the ones unsaid too,
and...the only few...made by you;
this time, fulfil it only if you please...
I have but left it
on you, for this promise to keep...

The bird I knew…
chirped ceaselessly
with wings gigantic, she flew;
hawks came for her,
she fought,
survived…wounded yet endured!

The bird I know,
still chirps…
with her eyes shining,
the colossal wings,
now range the silver lining…
soaring above the hawks,
she triumphs—eclipsing all odds…

I choose to be happy,
yes, it's a choice!
Just like the state of mind,
you can settle on this too!
Be kinder to yourself...
you are all you have.

I beam and look into eye
when faced with glitches,
for when the trail twitches...
you realise the block;
it's not always the key you need,
just analyse the lock.
Route to unbolt,
there—told!

Start from where you are,
do all you can...
try with all your will,
put all your might;
just creed in yourself,
it will turn out the way you covet!
Yes, it will...

Through the burning desire
effort will arise.
If the longing is ablaze,
you certainly will attain;
for all else—try excuses
they can sometimes save face…

To understand life
you do not necessarily need
a cognitive approach,
intuition usually can coach
what reasoning can withhold,
let the inner sense unfold!

Hold tight of destination
but be open to the routes,
don't be adamant...
if essential, take diversions...

Only if it is crucial enough
it won't seem tough
to cease the fire—you will come!

When you know your strength
not dwelling in it would be prudence,
focal is creating from it,
that's where the true forte is!

The purpose will arise
when awareness of self is high.
For only you know within
the texture of the passion
you are born to accomplish,
begin to know yourself,
you are your longest company...

Spirituality

When logic swirls you,
in dark, deep, deadly cyclone
amidst the scariest sea
it is only the faith,
that will take you to the shore and set free!

The breeze will whisper,
tossing your hair behind the ear,
just carefully, my dear,
listen…
close your eyes and smile,
embrace the breeze,
that just delivered you the sign!

You are the abundance,
if they turn away after consuming you,
they were but poor seekers.

Release yourself from the cage,
let the spirit unknot,
you don't have to know it all,
it's OK, my friend.
To leave some questions
as an unanswered call.
Lose yourself…
it's a recovery
from getting lost…

There are no rules...
but here is a cue,
just ask...
you shall have it,
just grip your belief.
What you say,
so shall be!

They say...
do not trust;
and open merely to the crust...
I probe...
then how can you say
you are in love
unless you surrender your faith...?

The usual retort...
they turn away...
in dismay...
I, however, again say...
sans the clouds, it won't rain,
you are not in love
unless, have surrendered your faith...

In the darkness,
amidst the vagueness,
when you see nothing with eyes…
and all when seems blank;
wait…
it is precisely then,
you see lucidly,
still not with the eyes…
but with the soul within,
clasp the moment
with regard and assent,
you have just found yourself…

Never in my imagination
or the foggiest notion,
I could have dared
to hold the thought…
that O' my Lord
I would meet you.
That you would confer
yourself upon the undeserving;
bequeathed I feel,
drenched in your love,
blessed in your refuge,
I become the worthy soul!

Silence…
the frozen silence,
usually comes to me,
the tryst is rather fascinating…
we both behold gently
the tricks of the sphere,
some waves fading,
and a few—too clear,
we often share, with time
what's woven in the mind,
enriching one another…
seeking nothing further,
that's when we confer,
without stating a word!
And then…we depart,
taking a passing, gradual leave,
nodding to meet yet again,
certainly not at the same place…!

Slowly, I walked to the graveyard,
and sat in front of you…
reasoning once again
but going for it anyway.
Yet Again…it is my need
to match the balance sheet,
witnessing what died
a little on the outer…
ahhh…more inside.
Then, the same story
you are once more to bury…

Looking at the sky,
I silently smile
knowing you stay in peace
the price is for me to keep,
in Some tales of love.
Lovers ensue separation;
I bow and accept,
counting it as
only His justice!

Prayers are beautiful,
they grant you a power,
in that instant
nothing remains unattainable.
Everything at that moment can be dealt
for you at least become true to yourself!
Prayers connect you to the Master,
my friend, pray often!

Breathing and believing
are quite similar,
you don't have to make an effort,
it is inherent...
you can't live without the first
and don't find a purpose
in absence of the latter...
it is the same, however...is it not?

Clouds create shapes,
often the one we want
in that blue,
the snow spreads in tune,
you can create likewise...
whatever you choose in life.
The shapes soon appear
once you overcome the fear!

The flame that burns in front of me...
spreading the fragrance in the room,
wordlessly says...

"I brighten up and dance,
to the notes that the breeze plays...
fire in me enlivens on the symphony it creates.
I witness the best shares of you,
you give away so much in solitude,
dissolving in night's darkest melancholy...
while you sly, when in company!"

continued...

Well, it also secretly spills...
where I lack the skills,
I know the flame laughs at me covertly,
just being discreet in front of me;

aren't you burnt when lit?
I ask, now she replies to unmask...

"It's not me that burns,
it's what's beneath me that does...
should it not?
is it not the law?

continued...

all the way, staying at the peak
purifying what contains me...
eternally remaining the most beautiful sight
to the observer's eyes...
bedecking every corner and shrine,
still should I wail and whine...?
Living graciously while alive?"

Only if I could be Water...
as pure, as serene,
sacred as nature,
the highest of all creation;
it beautifully penetrates
through any openness,
holds no shape, colour or place
prepared to be taken away...
never seeking its own identity,
I wish to possess
the art to be modest
while holding such prowess.

Only if I could be Water,
the texture—soft and smooth,
nothing from it
could remain aloof.
it enriches everything by touch,
ending all the search...
from nourishing the thirst
to comforting the fire...
could there be a fortune
with strength any higher?

Let me be whole,
don't divide me in fragments,
for when you categorise me,
you interpret me the way you choose to;
it is not me then...
you analyse a part
that's assigned by you.
it is anything but true...
stop!
Stop tearing me apart...
let me be whole!

continued...

I am not my name,
I am not the colour,
no—neither the place on map...
if you desire to know me and peel
come...come see how I feel—
how I do,
to what I do...
my place is—
where I want it to be...
when I bind and why I let lose...
just how I turn a conflict into truce...
in the middle of tears, why I manage a smile?
Like in desert, travels the Nile...
you will know me then...
...and yes, that would forever suffice!

As drops touch the soil,
my heart skips a beat
some strokes are felt deep inside.
The chords are played,
music erupts.
I know how frail…
my beloved rain,
you feel desolate;
for I have sensed the same…
albeit, now it is not the case…
I now await the drops…
when the clouds become dark,
instead of feeling lonely,
I prefer getting soaked,
still letting the chords play…

Eyes, wet with moisture…
perhaps frightened,
want to convey…
a message…
seeking a refuge
when no one could be of any use,
then…He listens,
like always…eyes don't see
yet feel and behold,
the warmth in the cold.

Eyes soaked once again,
with desire…
yearning to affiliate,
he listens again,
without fail…
now I am fervent in flame,
besotted…
all that I implored
now stands close…

Sunlight comes to greet
day after day…
we usually do not say hi,
neither do we appreciate it arrived,
yet it comes…
to get us on with the day,
we nevertheless fail to say
still soaking every ray;
how venal could we become…
and how charitable could it be?

Strand of hair,
c'mon, it is not fair…
you must stay,
where you belong…
not on the floor,
towel or tangled in teeth of a comb;
I want to look nice,
it is my need for you to shine…
please know your place,
after all…you are not THE human race…

Let it pass
the storm is hard
once it is settled...
you would know for sure
what the wind has taken
and what all it gifted...
let it pass!

Cherish the emotions you sense
they are in you for a reason...
listen and feel,
just breathe
they even do heal...

In the middle of the ocean
when I reached the depth,
my pain, hurt, disgrace—swept
I learnt the art to live,
let go...
whether it was a sign from above
or from underneath it sprout;
as much as it is crucial to breathe in—
more so is breathing out!

Hills possess a healing tendency
to its magnificence when you connect,
unveiled are powers of the mighty erect;
the ache is vaporised and the stings fade.
Go try…
just sit with them,
they will perform the rest…

The universe is smitten by you,
when you surrender the strings
and leave it all to it!
then the galaxies initiate
their submission to you!

Forgiveness is pricey
sprinkle it anyway;
it will liberate you,
even when not asked
free yourself from the sentence.